20 Tricks, Tips & Techniques on Successful Debt Collection

Krista T. Walsh, CFCP

The following publication is a compilation of Tricks, Tips & Techniques that are essential for successful debt management and prevention. It includes practical tactics and approaches for controlling your business's credit and collection department.

For my mentors
Thank you for believing in me when I didn't necessarily believe in myself

Table of Contents

20 Tricks, Tips & Techniques on Successful Debt Collection

1. Finding Mr. Right

Hiring someone to do your accounts receivable can prove to be a difficult task. The success of a company relies heavily on its credit policies and procedures, so carefully selecting the correct candidate to manage your credit department is of the utmost importance. A combination of the following skills sets is essential for choosing the right person.

Strong personality: This is mandatory in order to work in receivables management. While people not paying bills is not always the norm, your credit manager must be able to handle difficult situations and resolve conflict effectively while still maintaining a good relationship with your customer. People who cannot deal with constant confrontation and upset customers should not be considered for this position.

Organized: They must be able to keep detailed notes, including pay-dates, reminders, and agreements made between your company and your clients. This will aid you in future interactions, especially if the account has to be taken to court.

Customer service skills: As they will be dealing with your customers on a one-to-one basis in order to extend them credit or resolve a situation, personnel must excel in this area. A majority of your employee's duties will include handling different personalities, excuses and customer confrontations.

Patience and empathy: These character traits are essential, as ideally you would like to maintain the relationship with a customer by offering different payment options. In the unfortunate event that the relationship is not salvageable, your credit manager may have to take a more aggressive approach to recover the funds.

Investigation: Most often, in order to recover debt, you must locate a customer who has moved. Whether the customer is trying to hide from you, or has just mistakenly forgotten to give you a forwarding address, your employee must be keen in establishing their whereabouts. They must be able to form personal connections with sources in order to develop a trusting relationship. Acquiring information about is not always easy, but it can also assist in locating a person and thus result in a payment for your company.

Strong Negotiator: Your potential employee must be able to remain unbiased and develop a suitable settlement for both parties. This is essential when you want to maintain strong customer relations and secure future business.

A combination of all these characteristics is important when selecting a candidate who is going to successfully manage and maintain your accounts receivable. The future of your company could be in their hands.

2. The Four Cs of Extending Credit

As credit is considered to be one of our most important assets, as a creditor you should be careful in deciding to whom you are going to grant that privilege. When extending credit you want your customer to possess:

Collateral – Customers must be able to "back up" their loan with some type of asset that they can use as leverage.

Character – Customers should be able to provide you with financial or personal references that you are able to contact. Personal credit reports, background checks and written referral letters are all items to consider.

Career – Essentially you would like your customer to be employed or be aware of their source of income. If they are unemployed, how are they going to re-pay their debt to you? Pay stubs, a letter from their employer and proof of length of employment are important when making your decision to grant them credit.

Competence – People who display a general understanding of borrowing money and the consequences if re-payment terms are not met are going to be better candidates for extending credit services.

3. Extending Credit

Extending credit to customers, like most things, has its advantages and disadvantages. By extending credit to your customers you give them the option to purchase products or services today and pay for them at a later date. Whether your business accepts credit cards, personal cheques, or whether it invoices customers directly, extending credit is based on the assumption that customers have the funds to pay for the transaction.

The advantage of extending credit is that your customers will have the option to purchase your products right away instead of waiting to accumulate enough money to do so, thus bringing in more immediate business.

The disadvantage of extending credit to your customers is that that you do not necessarily get payment right away. Not receiving immediate payment can affect cash flow and therefore may not be suitable for your business.

You might also consider what will happen when the customers who have received invoices do not come forth and pay their bills, or send cheques that are NSF (non-sufficient funds)?

There are many reasons and/or excuses for not paying a bill. Knowing how to handle each situation and response is going to arm you with the necessary tools for positive results.

4. Creating Cash Flow

Every company struggles with the pressures of maintaining their cash flow. With proper governance and organization, companies should be able to easily ensure the management of their financial house.

Review your accounts receivable on a regular basis: Many business owners do not have the necessary training to completely understand the accounting side of their enterprise. Poor credit management is the top reason that businesses fail, so it is important to either learn the lingo or invest in a trusted accountant.

Develop a credit policy: Business owners (especially new business owners) can be so eager for a sale that they either forget to, or are too timid to review payment terms with a new client. The more up-front you are about your payment terms, the less likely a misunderstanding or delay in payment will occur.

Invest in your staff: Acquire the correct training to educate your staff. The more time you invest in your staff, the more results you will see.

Constant Contact: Persistence equals payment. You must keep customers aware that their debt is still outstanding and the payment is necessary. If you are not in constant contact the debt may be forgotten or viewed as less important.

Use your resources: Don't be afraid to out-source your accounts receivable. Not every company has a designated person to handle this aspect of the business. Make sure that you use a company with specifically trained and certified employees.

5. Keeping the Peace

In small communities it is difficult to not take receivables management personally. Having a hard-nosed or a tough approach to collections does not always yield the best, or most desirable results. Such attitudes can make a person less effective and decrease the chances of payment. Business owners must be careful not to offend or threaten their customers as client relationships are an important part of building and maintaining a business in any community.

Occasionally, a collector must be stern when explaining the current situation, but the most effective collectors never bully, threaten, or raise their voices. Instead they clearly explain the account situation, the potential actions and the consequences that may follow if payment is not received.

Keep in mind the following traits, so as to keep your customer on side, while still getting your overdue accounts paid.

Patience: Not everyone has the means to pay their past due account in its entirety. Most debtors are going to need your expert guidance in order to properly budget their existing debt. You have to be patient with them as you conceive an appropriate payment plan that is going to lessen their debt load and result in payment.

Persistence: The "out-of-sight, out of mind" mentality is quite common when attempting to collecting debt. If you keep persisting, you have a better chance of being paid when the money becomes available. Keeping the account fresh in their memory is an important tool to recovering debt

Empathetic: Being sensitive to the debtor's current situation will most likely aide in your attempts in getting paid. Most people have full intentions to repay debt, but, due to unforeseen circumstances, have fallen behind on their bills. Working together to resolve the debt will instil proper money management and better the individual for future financial transactions.

Combining these three traits, patience, persistence and empathy will usually result in fewer receivables for your company, reduce stress and increase cash flow.

6. Accepting Personal Cheques

In our ever-changing virtual world, cash and cheques seem to be becoming obsolete. Business owners must decide if they are still willing to accept this method of payment.

Date on Cheque: Make sure that the date on the cheque is within six months of issue. All cheques over this period are considered "stale dated" and institutions will not honour them.

Examine before cashing: Note the written amount on the cheque as well as the numbered amount. If there is a discrepancy between them, the bank will honour the written amount only.

Check Memo: Be careful of endorsing "Paid in Full" or any other memo on a personal/business cheque. As you are accepting it as payment, it could be used against you if it is only a partial payment or the incorrect amount.

Returned Cheque Fees: Ensure that your customers know how much you charge if their cheque is returned for any reason. Most companies charge a $50.00 administration fee. The type of customer who complains about this fee is the not the customer from whom you want to accept such methods of payment.

7. Protecting Yourself – Credit Card Safety

With online and telephone scams becoming more common in today's society, we cannot be too careful in protecting our personal credit. Keep your credit information and credit cards away from:

Children: Websites sometimes require a credit card and the user to be over 18 years old to access it. With children, pre-teens, and teenagers becoming increasingly dependent on technology, they are constantly introduced to websites that require credit card information for access.

Family/Friends: A lot of cases of identity theft are committed by someone who is known to the victim.

Employees: If you run a business and want to pay your bills by credit card, do not give access to your hired help. If something was to go wrong in the business, they could become spiteful and use your credit card and/or personal information fraudulently.

Telemarketers: Unless it is a reputable company that can identify itself adequately, do not give out credit card details or other personal information on the phone until you are 100% certain. There are many phone fraudsters who claim to be an honourable company. Never give your account number to an unknown person over the phone. Beware of anyone who says you've won a valuable prize and you need to give them your credit card number to claim it.

Never provide your credit card by email, text message or instant messaging format. This is not a secure, trusted way to transfer funds. Always research prior to purchasing to determine if a merchant uses a secure website for all business and monetary transactions.

You should always safeguard your personal information, including your social insurance number, your personal identification number (PIN), your date of birth, mother's maiden name, address and telephone number. Merchants should never require your address or telephone number, unless they will be shipping goods to your home.

8. Friend or Foe?

It is often difficult for a small business owner to play the role of the friendly sales agent, as well as the adamant credit manager while maintaining a relationship the customer. Unfortunately, when extending credit there is no definite way to guarantee payment. With a proper credit policy in place, this should decrease receivables and make it less likely for the business owner to turn into the enemy when faced with collecting the overdue account.

Many business owners, especially new business owners, are so eager for a sale that they neglect signing documents or discussing payment. The business does not want to offend the new customer by asking for a method of payment. They fear that if it is difficult for a customer to obtain credit, they will take their business elsewhere. Lack of proper credit policy is the main reason that businesses have overdue accounts. Small businesses are infamously guilty of having a weak or non-existent collection policy.

Some businesses have a policy but use it inconsistently, this yields less than favourable results. As one of the keys to success of any business, receivables management must be taken into consideration when venturing out as an entrepreneur. Unfortunately this key element is often overlooked as the entrepreneur's attention is pulled in different directions.

If you obtain as much information as possible from the customer when extending this credit recovery of the account is more likely if it becomes past due. In order to successfully manage debt, it is customary to ask potential customers for credit references. In smaller communities it is suggested that you network with fellow companies to, creating a mutual exchange of information. Most companies are quite willing to share information on past delinquents to help you to learn from their mistakes.

9. Credit Policy Musts

- Determine to whom you are going to extend credit (i.e. anyone, new customers, etc.).
- Decide a suitable credit limit. This could vary depending on the customer.
- Ensure all staff members are aware of the credit policy and are aware that it MUST be enforced.
- Decide upon the terms? I.e. 30 days? 60 days? Pay upon receipt?
- Decide upon penalties to be imposed if an account becomes past due.
- What actions are you going to take when there is non-payment?
- In rural areas, recovering outstanding debt becomes another challenge for the striving business owner.

As you strive to build your customer base, it is suggested that another employee who is not a customer service representative takes on the daunting task of collections. This delegation will enable the owner to maintain strong relations with the customer while still enforcing the recovery of the debt. In most cases this is where a collection professional or third party agency is required. The collection expert may opt to use the "Soft Touch" approach to recover an account while keeping a positive relationship between the client and debtor. This non-aggressive method gently encourages the debtor to reveal the reasons for the overdue account. On most occasions it requires the debtor to confide their financial situation to the collection professional and together devise a payment plan suitable for both parties.

Information Wanted When Extending Credit
- Request a credit check on your customer.
- Ask for more than a post office box. Post office boxes can be changed or closed so ask for a civic or street address.
- Ask for a customer's date of birth and/or social security number. This will help you to trace them in the future.

- Hold two people responsible for the debt by asking for both spouses' names, for example.
- Inquire about their employment history. How are they going to pay you if they are under/unemployed?

Remember: The customer who has a problem with getting their credit checked is the customer that you **DO NOT** want.
Every business must develop and maintain a strong credit policy. Each time a customer leaves a business with goods or services, that business takes on the role of a bank.

Before Submitting an Overdue Account to a Third Party
Determine if the debt is collectable. As the debt ages, the chance of recovering the debt will decrease dramatically.

Attempt to contact the debtor by phone and set a deadline for payment.

Send a final notice informing the debtor that you have been forced to forward the account to a third party and/or to take legal action.

10. Effective Collection Techniques

Professional Collectors or Accounts Receivable staff are always looking for new methods to use while trying to recover a debt. With the following popular techniques, the professional collector can work as a part of a team, individually or a combination of the two in order to achieve success in debt recovery.

The Policeman: This joint questioning technique is a collection tactic which plays a team of two collection agents against each other. Each team member takes an opposing approach to try to solidify payment from the debtor.

When the Collection agent takes a very aggressive, sometimes threatening approach, they are instantly dubbed the 'Bad Cop'. This strong-armed approach creates a negative interaction between the debtor and agent and usually paves the way for the 'Good Cop'.

As the stage is set for the 'Good Cop', it is now their turn to act sympathetically: they appear supportive, understanding, and generally show sympathy for the subject. The good cop will also defend the subject to the bad cop. The subject may feel he can cooperate with the good cop out of trust and/or fear of the bad cop. The debtor may then seek to rectify the overdue account as a result of the bond that was formed with the 'Good Cop' and shows they are willing to cooperate.

The Chinese Torturer: In ancient times it was believed that the Chinese used a method called "Water Torture" to get results. The tactic used in obtaining results was credited to the ongoing persistence. This is a method to consistently deliver the message that the debt is serious and you are not going to cease efforts until resolved.

The key part of Chinese Water Torture is that the water drop was made to be randomly timed. Thus, the collection agent must adjust his schedule so that the debtor does not know when the next contact will be made.

The Vacuum Cleaner Salesman: This personal approach is usually used when most other attempts in making contact has failed. Catching a debtor off-guard without making an appointment, leads them to believe that you will stop at nothing to get this debt paid. Often the fear of a collection agent randomly visiting will result in payment.

The Clergyman: This soft approach is also known as the 'velvet touch'. This is used when trying to recover an account while keeping the relationship between the client and debtor. This non-aggressive method pushes the debtor to reveal the reason for the overdue account. Mostly it requires the debtor to confide their financial situation to the collection agent so that together they can devise a payment plan suitable for both parties.

Once you have determined which approach will be the most effective with the debtor, you will be better prepared for any objections the debtor may present. Learning how to approach each debtor individually will dramatically increase your chances of collecting the debt.

11. Collection Calls

Be prepared: Make sure that you have reviewed all the account information prior to picking up the phone. This will equip you with the necessary details of the account including any previous disputes or queries.

Always professional: Even if the customer becomes upset, you must remain calm. Focus on keeping the customer on the line while discovering the reason for non-payment.

Stick to the facts: You can only present the facts of the situation. Never assume other details that are not present or irrelevant to the account.

Confirm payment: After you have overcome the obstacles and excuses presented by the customer, you can then work out a suitable payment plan. Ensure that you set a payment amount, date and time before you end the conversation.

Follow up: If the agreed payment date is longer than one week, then a follow up or reminder may be necessary. A quick courtesy phone call or email is sufficient to keep them aware that you are expecting payment.

12. The ABC's of Handling Excuses

When dealing with overdue accounts, it can seem like there is no end to customer excuses. If we do not handle them correctly, we often hang up the phone and wish we had of asked something else. By following this simple ABC plan, a collector has a greater chance of recovering the outstanding debt.

A – Ask Questions: When a person is lying, they will become more and more uncomfortable. Eventually making an effort to get this bill paid is less work than dealing with your questions. Keep detailed notes on every contact with the customer—if they are lying they may have a different story than they had originally told you. Most times catching them in a lie will result in payment.

B – Backbone: Do not let the debtor hang up the phone without making payment arrangements and deadlines. Do not settle for "I will pay that sometime this month/week". Give them a deadline and make sure that this is confirmed before you hang up. Use lines like "So you have confirmed that you will make payment on or before next Friday at 3pm." In some cases a follow up reminder is needed if you are giving a deadline of 2 weeks or more.

Don't sympathize with the debtor and try to relate. This will make them think that you "understand" and they may not have to pay the bill. Just because they are going through a rough time, does not excuse them from paying a bill. Try to work out a suitable payment plan until they have stabilized their financial situation.

C – Control: Keep control of the conversation. Keep focused on the debt. Do not let the debtor stall the conversation with their personal history. DO NOT let it get personal.

Sometimes it is inevitable to avoid the debtors long drawn out excuses. They give you a long in-depth story of the crises in their life. In this case, let them talk. When they are finally finished take a moment or two, and response should be "I am sorry to hear that, but let's stay focused on the debt itself and try to work out a suitable payment plan".

Even when dealing with family or friends, you can't let them get upset by you doing your job.

Most frequently used debtor excuse:
"I am going through a rough time right now"

13. L.E.A.R.N. to Diffuse the Irate Customer

It is inevitable that you are going to engage with a less-than-happy customer at some point. Possessing the skills in order to properly diffuse the situation will benefit you by easing the situation and potentially keeping your customer. It's easy to "L.E.A.R.N." from our conversations:

Listen: Most times customers just want to be heard. Let them vent, cry and sulk without interruption.

Empathise: This will help you connect with the customer and maintain the relationship.

Ask questions: The better the questions you ask the more able you will be to evaluate the situation and efficiently resolve the complaint.

Remain calm: Nothing escalates the conversation more than trying to talk over or interrupt a person when they are ranting about the unfairness they have experienced. Instead lower your voice and they will match you with a softer tone.

Negotiate: Everyone likes the feeling of winning. Offering a customer a discounted price, a promotional item, or even a small gift card will most often turn a negative situation into a positive one.

14. Debtor or Animal?

These two "creatures" have more in common than you would think. When faced with a collections agent, some debtors will often display familiar characteristics associated with some well-known animals. Nature has developed different mechanisms to communicate with animals, and so must the collections agent when dealing with these types of debtors.

The Chameleon: This type of debtor is the hardest to collect from. They will do everything that they can to avoid contact. They use the "out-of-sight-out-of-mind" mentality. Chameleons are known for their ability to change their color and disguise themselves. These debtors will often pretend they are not home, they will stop answering their phone, and sometimes they will even hide behind people or objects when you see them in public.

On the rare occasions when you do make contact, the chameleons will try everything to get you off track. They will try to direct the focus on less important circumstances surrounding the account. For example; they may suggest that it is your fault that the letter was sent to the wrong address; or perhaps your company was not supposed to cash a check until a certain day; or maybe they never got your messages because you were leaving them at the wrong number. The chameleon is very talented at this and the list seems endless at times.

Solution: Remain focused. No matter what the excuse, no matter how impressive the disappearing act, no matter what the disguise is, you must take control of the conversation and keep it until your focus becomes the most important one. Be persistent.

Ant: This debtor is a hard worker. They are by nature and purpose very proud, and they will not easily ask for help. They try to go to work every day, and they honestly believe that if they work just a little harder they will make the money necessary to pay off the debt. The problem is there is ALWAYS something that comes up and takes their money. Working harder and longer does not solve the problem: it just makes them more tired and less likely to be receptive to help. The ant has lost focus despite the best intentions.

Solution: Show respect to these debtors and gently supply them with ideas on how to better budget. If possible or necessary, let the debtors think it was their idea.

Laughing Hyena: The hyena laughs when being pursued or when dealing with great fear. It is an escape mechanism. The hyena never plans an attack, but likes to take the route with the least effort and risk. This type of debtor is not exactly grounded in reality. They believe that it will all work out. Tomorrow. Somehow. They believe that the payment date at the end of the month is fine because the money will just appear from somewhere. If they do not have the money today, it will be here tomorrow.

Solution: Guide the debtor in the direction that will yield the best results. Begin by asking questions that will allow the debtor to understand the reality of the situation. The debtor must make a workable and realistic plan, AND STICK TO IT.

Pot Bellied Pig: This debtor will probably throw some sort of temper tantrum. During the conversation, it is most likely that they will fuss, yell, cry and vent in some dramatic display of emotion. Like the potbellied pig, they can seem stubborn and unreasonable. For the collections agent, it is imperative to know where this frustration is coming from. This debtor is likely reacting this way because they are mad at themselves, their situation and their financial inadequacies. They want to take care of the debt but have no idea how.

Solution: Explain to the debtor that the frustration is normal, that you empathize with the situation, and that you are willing to work together to find a successful answer.

It is important to determine the type of debtor that you are facing in order to be most effective. Once you have determined the debtors' style, you will be more prepared for the reactions, and you will have a better opportunity to overcome any objections that the debtors present while trying to repay their debt. After we determine which animal we are dealing with, our chances of collecting the debt will increase.

15. Collecting During Christmas

There is no doubt that with today's economic state companies are going to find it difficult to collect in the weeks before Christmas. Businesses definitely don't want to be labeled as Scrooge, but still want to recover those funds owing. Instead of the constant negative connotation that is usually associated with the collection department, try utilizing these tips that may make Christmas come early for both parties.

Be Efficient: The first two weeks in December are critical for making contact and collecting overdue accounts. Most families like to take vacation and it will become increasingly difficult to collect as the days before Christmas dwindle. Assess your accounts and focus on collecting the ones that are going to be the most prosperous. Use your times wisely and stop putting effort into those uncollectible accounts.

Be a Secret Santa: Everyone loves a sign of good-faith during a stressful time. Try to negotiate smaller payments during the holiday season, in exchange for a larger payment in January. Debtors will often return this kind gesture with an increase in payments in the New Year.

Strike a Deal: Request that the debtor hands over their income tax return in the New Year. Since this is usually viewed as bonus income, it is not considered to be a loss, as it was usually never accounted for during their budgeting.

Rest up: Since financial problems can be the main cause of stress for people during this season, you may find that debtors are not going to take kindly to constant contact. Instead try taking the last week in December and first week in January as vacation. Give yourself a much-needed break to energize yourself. You will find that if you take time for yourself you will feel more rejuvenated and constructive in the New Year.

Enjoy the holidays. Remember no one on their death bed said that they wished they had spent more time at work.

BONUS – Personal Finance

16. Importance of Starting Young

Living in our ever-changing debt society, parents should begin teaching children about money, budgeting and saving while they are young. This will result in fiscally educated youngsters who have a head-start on financial responsibility.

Allowances: Popular techniques for allowances are based on a points system. As more points accumulate, the more rewards the child can receive. This tool is excellent in teaching the value of money and achieving goals. Giving children a weekly allowance will prepare them for being paid as an adult and is an effective way to teach them about money management.

Bank Accounts: Start at a young age. Having your children put money aside from their allowance teaches them to save and how easy it is to do so. Some financial institutions have incentives and programs available for young savers.

Birthday Presents or Birthday Investments: Suggest to family members that they make small monetary donations to your child instead of traditional presents. Depositing this money directly into your child's bank account means they will be able to watch their savings grow!

Setting goals: Together set a goal that your child would like to save for: a specific toy, trip, or even a movie night. This teaches responsibility with money, budgeting, and patience to wait until they have all of the money to purchase the item.

17. Smarter Banking

Cut Transportation costs: Using online or telephone banking can save time, cut down on transportation costs and often save on service fees. Did you know most of the time it costs extra to have a person wait on you in-person?

Avoid Other ATMs: When using an ATM from another bank, you may be charged for the transaction plus a service fee. By using your own bank you avoid these hidden charges.

Seniors/Students: Some institutions offer seniors and student no fee chequing accounts. Make sure you are aware that as soon as you are not a student, you could rack up account charges without realizing.

No Account Fees: When opening a "No Fee" account make sure that you read the fine print. You may find that there are no fees only when you hold a certain balance or higher (some banks use a minimum balance of $1000).

Review your accounts: View your account history daily. Save your receipts and double check the charges with your online banking. There's nothing worse than a hefty overdraft fee due to negligence.

Practice effective online security: When shopping or making transaction over the internet, do not use obvious personal words likes names, birthdays, or pets in combination with a single number as these passwords are easier to crack than whole phrases.

18. Digging out of Debt

Does the start of a New Year often find you digging out of debt? We are not only tunnelling ourselves out of a blanket of snow at this time of year, but we are also trying to dig our way out of debt. With the excessive spending that occurred in December, it is now time to pick up a shovel and burrow a way out.

Get a Tow: Not everyone can maneuver out of a snow bank unassisted. Request the assistance of professional credit counselling services. Certified not-for-profit agencies have the expertise to help you carefully manage your finances when you find yourself under a 'snow bank" of debt.

Do Not Panic: Make a New Year's resolution. This is the best time to sit down and plan your budget for the up-coming year. A written plan is a necessary step in preparing your finances for the future. A lack of necessary budgeting skills is one of the major reasons that people over spend and eventually become bankrupt.

Control Yourself: Stick to the bare essentials and think before you make your purchases. Try to keep your spending minimal while you weather the storm. Even though you are trying to dig yourself out, try always to make more than your minimum payments. You will never shovel yourself out if you opt to only make the smallest payment.

19. Identity Theft

With today's rapidly growing online society, we are faced with a new type of robbery. Identity theft is growing throughout our nation. By taking certain precautions to prevent it from happening, we are protecting our greatest asset.

Track yourself: By frequently using online search engines such as "Google" and "Bing" you will be able to monitor your online presence.

Monitor your personal credit report: Check your credit report on a regular basis. If you visit your local offices (Trans Union or Equifax) they are required to provide you with your personal credit report at no charge. You will be able to identify any discrepancies and act on them immediately. There are also many online sites available where you can access your credit reports for free or for a small fee.

Practice effective online security: When shopping or making transaction over the internet, do not use obvious personal words likes names, birthdays, or pets in combination with a single number as these passwords are easier to crack than whole phrases.

Hide personal information: When using social networking sites, make sure that your personal information is not accessible to the public. Publicly viewed addresses, dates of birth, and workplaces can make it very inviting for identity thieves.

The better we get at recognizing identity theft, the more adept we become in minimizing the personal damage.

20. Money Management Tips

Successful Money Management Tips: Here are some suggestions to get you started in your constant battle of reducing your debt load. If you have a strategy in place, then you are more likely to succeed in driving down your debt.

Budget Buddy: Much like a fitness routine, try to find an 'accountability partner' to help you stay on track with your budget. They will be able to assist in reinforcing your goals and give you gentle correction.

Cash Allowance: Only withdrawal enough cash to last you for the week. This will make you think about what you are buying instead of handing over your debit/credit card for transactions. This will assist you in budgeting for the week and tracking where you are spending recklessly. Plan on saving anything that is left over at the end of the week

Highest Interest = Highest Priority: Give your bill with the highest interest your main priority. You don't want to be caught just paying out the interest. Make sure that you always pay more than your minimum payments. If you only make your minimum credit card payments each month, it will take much more time to get your balance to zero. The longer you drag out payment on this debt, the more interest you are going to pay.

Contact Me:
I would be pleased to hear any feedback you have.
Please contact me at:
Email:
info@kccollect.com

Website:
www.kccollect.com
www.kristatwalsh.com

Facebook:
www.facebook.com/kristawalshprofessionaldevelopment
www.facebook.com/kc.collect

Twitter:
@kccollect

Regular Mail:
PO Box 1616
Montague, PE C0A 1R0

Phone: (902) 838 7000